Animal Opposites

Soft
and
HARD

An Animal Opposites Book

by Nathan Olson

Capstone press

Mankato, Minnesota

Some animals are covered with soft, fluffy fur. Others live inside rock-hard shells. Let's learn about soft and hard by looking at animals around the world.

Soft

Kittens are soft pets. They lick their fur to keep it clean and fuzzy.

Pet hermit crabs live inside hard shells.
When they grow too big, they find new shells.

Soft

Baby swans are covered with soft, fluffy feathers called down.

Armadillos are covered with hard, bony plates called armor.

Armadillos are very good diggers. They use their claws to dig up a meal of bugs.

Soft

Butterflies flutter with soft wings. They fly from plant to plant looking for nectar.

Butterfly wings have the same pattern on the top two wings and the bottom two wings.

HARD

Beetle bodies are protected.
They have hard outer coverings
called exoskeletons.

Soft

Earthworms have long bodies that are soft and squishy.

An earthworm has no arms, legs, or eyes. But it does have a mouth. An earthworm can eat one-third of its own body weight in a single day.

Snails have squishy bodies too.
But they live inside hard shells.
They carry their shells with
them as they slime along.

Soft

Sea sponges are soft like foam cushions. Some people add soap and use them in the bathtub.

The hard shells of clams open and close like a treasure chest.

Giant clams can grow to be 4 feet (1 meter) long.

Soft

Puppy paws are soft and furry.
Paws help puppies walk, run, and dig.

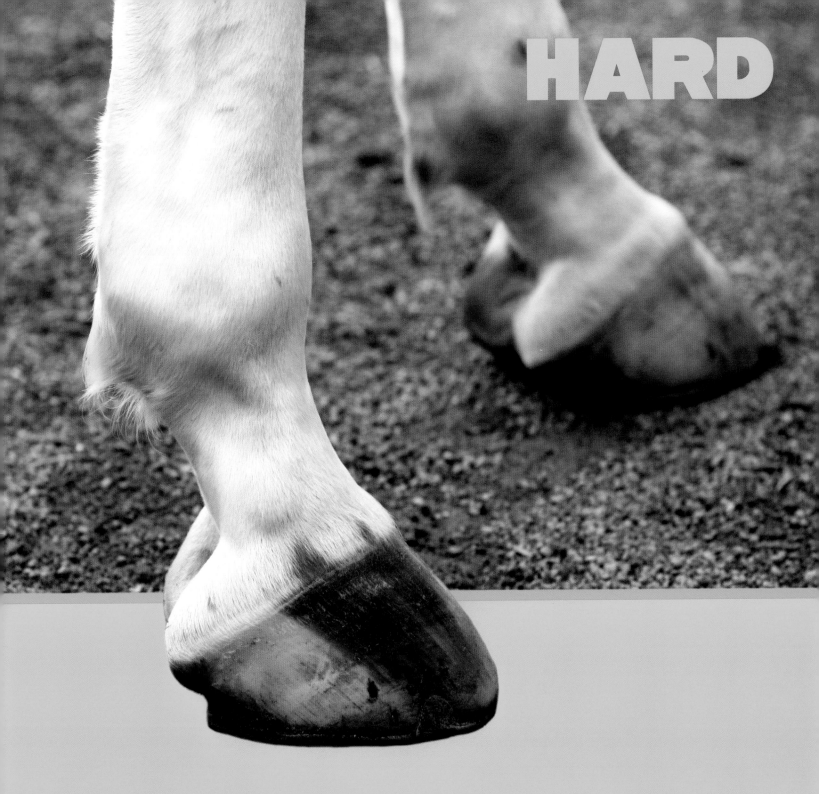

Horse hooves are hard and strong.
Hooves help horses trot, gallop, and jump.

Soft

Moose antlers are covered with soft velvet in spring. Moose rub their antlers on tree trunks to scrape off the velvet.

16

HARD

The hard horns on rams' heads
are tough. They use their horns
to ram their enemies.

Soft

The tips of zebra tails are made of soft, stringy hairs. Zebras use their tails to swat away flies and other bugs.

The tips of rattlesnake tails have hard scales. Rattlesnakes shake their tails to make a warning noise before they bite.

Soft

A horse's muzzle is soft and smooth. Big nostrils give horses a great sense of smell.

Woodpeckers use
their hard beaks to
make holes in trees.

Soft

Llamas need their soft hair to keep warm. Their coat protects them in the cold mountains.

Rhinos need their hard horns to stay cool. They use them to dig up water and mud in dry places.

The horn of a rhinoceros is made from the same material as your fingernails and hair.

Soft

Arctic hares have soft fur that turns white in winter. They match the snow to stay safe.

Turtles don't need to change color. They live in hard shells that protect them.

Some animals have soft fur or feathers to keep them warm or dry. Other animals have hard shells or skin to stay safe.

What kinds of soft
and hard animals
live near you?

Did You Know?

Can you look left and right at the same time? You could if you were a horse! A horse can move each eye in a different direction.

Male rhinos use their horns to fight each other. The horns are sharp enough to poke through another rhino's tough skin.

You can tell the difference between a hare and a rabbit by looking at their babies. Hares are born with their eyes open. They also have fur at birth. Rabbits are born blind and without fur.

Llama hair can be white, gray, brown, or black. The outer hair on a llama is used to make rugs and ropes. The undercoat is very soft and is used to make clothes.

As chicks and ducklings grow, tougher outer feathers grow in over the down. But the down underneath keeps birds warm in cold weather or cold water.

Glossary

armor (AR-mur) — bones, scales, and skin that some animals have on their body for protection; an armadillo's armor is small plates of bone covered with skin.

claw (KLAW) — a hard, curved nail on the foot of an animal or bird

down (DOUN) — the soft feathers of a bird

enemy (EN-uh-mee) — a person or animal that wants to harm or destroy another

exoskeleton (eks-oh-SKEL-uht-uhn) — the hard outer shell of an insect; the exoskeleton covers and protects the insect.

muzzle (MUHZ-uhl) — an animal's nose, mouth, and jaws

nectar (NEK-tur) — a sweet liquid that some insects collect from flowers and eat as food

slime (SLIME) — to move along at a slow pace, leaving a trail of a slippery substance

Read More

Arps, Melissa. *Opposites.* School Days. New York: Random House Children's Books, 2006.

Bullard, Lisa. *Smooth and Rough: An Animal Opposites Book.* A+ Books: Animal Opposites. Mankato, Minn.: Capstone Press, 2006.

Got, Yves. *Sam's Opposites.* San Francisco: Chronicle Books, 2003.

Internet Sites

FactHound offers a safe, fun way to find Internet sites related to this book. All of the sites on FactHound have been researched by our staff.

Here's how:

1. Visit *www.facthound.com*

2. Choose your grade level.

3. Type in this book ID **1429612134** for age-appropriate sites. You may also browse subjects by clicking on letters, or by clicking on pictures and words.

4. Click on the **Fetch It** button.

FactHound will fetch the best sites for you!

Index

32

A+ Books are published by Capstone Press,
1710 Roe Crest Drive, North Mankato, Minnesota 56003.
www.capstonepub.com

 Books published by Capstone Press are manufactured with paper
containing at least 10 percent post-consumer waste.

Library of Congress Cataloging-in-Publication Data
Olson, Nathan.
  Soft and hard: an animal opposites book / by Nathan Olson.
    p. cm. — (A+ books. Animal opposites)
  Includes bibliographical references and index.
  ISBN-13: 978-1-4296-1213-5 (hardcover)
  ISBN-10: 1-4296-1213-4 (hardcover)
  1. Animals — Juvenile literature. 2. Body covering (Anatomy) — Juvenile literature.
I. Title. II. Series.
QL941.O47 2008
590 — dc22   2007036220

Summary: Brief text introduces the concepts of soft and hard, comparing some of the world's
softest and hardest animals.

Credits
Heather Adamson and Megan Peterson, editors; Veronica Bianchini and
  Renée T. Doyle, designers; Wanda Winch, photo researcher

Photo Credits
Art Life Images/Georgie Holland, 13; Corbis/Royalty-Free, 17, 18, 23; iStockphoto/Devon
Stephens, 9; iStockphoto/Hedda Gjerpen, 15; Jupiterimages/Radius Images, 7;
Shutterstock/Alex Kuzovlev, 11; Shutterstock/Anna Chelnokova, 1 (middle), 3 (top);
Shutterstock/Annette, 14; Shutterstock/Arkadiy Yarmolenko, 20; Shutterstock/Bodil1955,
29; Shutterstock/Cathy Keifer, 8; Shutterstock/Christian Musat, 27 (top right); Shutterstock/
David Anderson, 10; Shutterstock/Edwin van Wier, 1 (right), 26 (top); Shutterstock/Eric
Isselee, 3 (middle); Shutterstock/Frank B. Yuwono, 5; Shutterstock/Gertjan Hooijer, 21 (tree);
Shutterstock/Jeff R. Clow, cover (armadillo), 27 (bottom); Shutterstock/Jenny Horne, 6;
Shutterstock/Jessica Bilen, 16; Shutterstock/John Bell, 19; Shutterstock/Libby J. Hansen, 26
(bottom); Shutterstock/Lincoln Rogers, 3 (bottom); Shutterstock/Nancy Kennedy, 2 (bottom);
Shutterstock/Nicolas Raymond, 22; Shutterstock/Robynrg, cover (bunny); Shutterstock/
Shawn Hine, 27 (top left); Shutterstock/Styve Reineck, 12–13; Shutterstock/Suponev
Vladimir Mihajlovich, 4; Shutterstock/Tim Zurowski, 21 (woodpecker); Shutterstock/Wendy
Sue Gilman, 1 (left), 2 (top); Shutterstock/Wikus Otto, 25; SuperStock, Inc./age fotostock, 24

Note to Parents, Teachers, and Librarians
This Animal Opposites book uses full-color photographs and a nonfiction format
to introduce children to the concepts of soft and hard. *Soft and Hard* is designed to
be read aloud to a pre-reader or to be read independently by an early reader.
Photographs help listeners and early readers understand the text and concepts
discussed. The book encourages further learning by including the following sections:
Did You Know?, Glossary, Read More, Internet Sites, and Index. Early readers may
need assistance using these features.

Printed in the United States of America in North Mankato, Minnesota.
012014   007957R